First World War
and Army of Occupation
War Diary
France, Belgium and Germany

40 DIVISION
119 Infantry Brigade
Prince of Wales's (North Staffordshire Regiment)
12th Battalion
10 June 1918 - 4 June 1919

WO95/2606/5

The Naval & Military Press Ltd
www.nmarchive.com
Published in association with The National Archives

Published by

The Naval & Military Press Ltd

Unit 10 Ridgewood Industrial Park,

Uckfield, East Sussex,

TN22 5QE England

Tel: +44 (0) 1825 749494

www.naval-military-press.com

www.nmarchive.com

This diary has been reprinted in facsimile from the original. Any imperfections are inevitably reproduced and the quality may fall short of modern type and cartographic standards.

© Crown Copyright
Images reproduced by permission of The National Archives, London, England, 2015.

Contents

Document type	Place/Title	Date From	Date To
Heading	WO95/2606/5 12 Battalion North Staffordshire Regiment.		
Heading	40th Division 119th Infy Bde 12th Bn Nth Stafford Regt Jun 1918-Jun 1919 Formed in France June 1918.		
Heading	War Diary of 12th Garr Battn. North Stafford Regt From 10th June 1918 to 30th June 1918 Volume I.		
War Diary	Broxeele.	10/06/1918	15/06/1918
War Diary	Le Paradis	16/06/1918	22/06/1918
War Diary	Staples Area U.10.c.26.81.27.	23/06/1918	24/06/1918
War Diary	Staples Area.	25/06/1918	30/06/1918
Heading	War Diary 12th Battn, North Stafford Regt. from July 1st 1918 to July 31st 1918 (Volume II).		
War Diary	Staple.	01/07/1918	10/07/1918
War Diary	Hazebrouke.	11/07/1918	14/07/1918
War Diary	Staple.	15/07/1918	16/07/1918
War Diary	Hazebruck	17/07/1918	18/07/1918
War Diary	Borre.	19/07/1918	21/07/1918
War Diary	Curfew House.	22/07/1918	25/07/1918
War Diary	Strazeele Station.	26/07/1918	31/07/1918
Heading	War Diary 12th Battn. North, Stafford. Regt. from 1st August 1918 to 31st August 1918 (Volume III).		
War Diary	Borre.	01/08/1918	01/08/1918
War Diary	Staple.	02/08/1918	31/08/1918
War Diary	Sheet 36 A N.E Swartenbroock.	01/09/1918	03/09/1918
War Diary	Pont Wemeau	04/09/1918	05/09/1918
War Diary	Steenwerk Switch.	06/09/1918	06/09/1918
War Diary	Nippon Bend.	07/09/1918	07/09/1918
War Diary	Nieppe System.	08/09/1918	08/09/1918
War Diary	Pont de Nieppe.	09/09/1918	13/09/1918
War Diary	Grand Beaumart.	13/09/1918	20/09/1918
War Diary	Hazebrouck.	21/09/1918	26/09/1918
War Diary	Meuniers.	27/09/1918	29/09/1918
War Diary	Nieppe.	30/09/1918	30/09/1918
War Diary	Nieppe Sheet 36. N.W.	30/09/1918	30/09/1918
Miscellaneous Operation(al) Order(s)	Operation Order No. 9 Battn No Staff Regt.		
Heading	War Diary 12th Battn North Staffs Regt. Vol. 5 From 1-10-18 To 31-10-18.		
War Diary	Nieppe.	01/10/1918	02/10/1918
War Diary	Houplines.	03/10/1918	31/10/1918
Heading	12th Bn. North Staffords. War Diary. Vol. VI. From: 1/11/18 To 30/11/18.		
Miscellaneous	Bn.		
War Diary		01/11/1918	30/11/1918
War Diary		25/11/1918	25/11/1918
Heading	12th Bn North Stafford Regt. War Diary Vol. VII from:- 1st Dec 18 To:- 31st Dec 18.		
War Diary	Croix.	01/12/1918	31/12/1918
War Diary	In The Field.	01/01/1919	31/01/1919

Heading	12th Bn. N. Staffs. Regt. War Diary Vol IX. from 1/2/19 To 28/2/19.		
War Diary	Croix Nord.	01/02/1919	08/02/1919
War Diary	Croix.	09/02/1919	25/02/1919
War Diary	Croix Nord.	26/02/1919	28/02/1919
Heading	12th Battalion North Staffs Regt. War Diary Vol X from 1/3/19 To 31/3/19.		
War Diary	Croix France.	01/03/1919	31/03/1919
Heading	War Diary 12 Bn N. Staff Regt Month of April 1919 Vol 11.		
War Diary	Croix.	01/04/1919	04/06/1919

WO 95/2606/5
12 Battalion North Staffordshire Regiment

40TH DIVISION
119TH INFY BDE

12TH BN NTH STAFFORD REGT

JUN 1918-JUN 1919

Formed in France June 1918

Confidential

War Diary
of
12th (Serv.) Battn. North Stafford Regt

From 10th June 1918 to 30th June 1918.

Volume I

Army Form C. 2118.

WAR DIARY
or
INTELLIGENCE SUMMARY.
(Erase heading not required.)

Place	Date	Hour	Summary of Events and Information	Remarks and references to Appendices
Broxeele	10/6/18		Following orders received from O.C. Reinforcements, Lt Col Grogan G.M., D.S.O. R.I. Regt proceeded to Watten, thence to Broxeele - Reported to 120th Brigade and billeted at Broxeele - Under his command were 4 Officers (Adjutant, Asst Adjutant, Transport Officer, Reinforcements) ST 1040R	49/1
"	11/6/18		T.O. went to Abbeville to draw first line transport, Q.M received first consignment of stores including 4 Lewis guns - began arrangements for billets of Battalion at Broxeele	49/1
"	12/6/18		Kit Inspection of H.Q Coy T Selection for Clerks - completing arrangements for billets	49/1
"	13/6/18		Return of Officers re - G.O. to Brigade HQ	49/1
"	14/6/18		Orders that Battⁿ would arrive at 2 A.M. 15/6/18 - at 11.45 P.M. Received orders that Battⁿ transferred to 119th Brigade T would move from 16th	JW

WAR DIARY
or
INTELLIGENCE SUMMARY.

(Erase heading not required.)

Army Form C. 2118.

Place	Date	Hour	Summary of Events and Information	Remarks and references to Appendices
Broxeele	14/4/18		to Le Paradis	A/C
"	15/4/18		4 Companies (W. garrison Bn - Capt E.W. Butler, V - Captain A.R.O. Rawlins, W - Capt Reeve Smith & X - Capt O.C. Newcombe) arrived from Pie. Duigny (IV Army) at Watton at 4 P.M. and marched to Broxe- -eele to billets arranged for. T.O. arrived back with amended scale of transport	A/C
Le Paradis	16/4/18		Battalion moved to Le Paradis arriving 12.30 P.M. - H.Q. in village and Companies billeted at farms & villages in vicinity - various returns obtained from Companies of Personnel & deficiencies - M.O. (Capt. Fleshing) joined for duty - visited by Brigadier fierce - Company Comdgrs & H.Q. Officers inspected trenches.	A/C
"	17/4/18		Battalion inspected by Brig. Gen. at Nieurlet in previous ret-	A/C

Army Form C. 2118.

WAR DIARY
or
INTELLIGENCE SUMMARY.
(Erase heading not required.)

Place	Date	Hour	Summary of Events and Information	Remarks and references to Appendices
Il Pardis	17/6/18		The same place in afternoon by Dunning Peraine - 2/Lt Weatherall joined for duty.	4857
"	18/6/18		Training began - 6 hours (Platoon Drill, P.T. & B.F. arms & Scouting) by Companies - Orderly Room at 1-30 - Names obtained from Companies of Subaltern Officers & O.R. for courses in gas, Lewis gun & Signalling - Names for S/B taken - arrangements made for instruction in P.T. & B.F. of Company instructors - 5 Sub. Officers proved for duty - Class for instruction in Lewis gun began under Lt Alles, 17Corps. Signalling under 2/Lt Ward, 73 Company - visited by Brig Genl.	AW
"	19/6/18		Training by Companies in France (P.T. & B.F. Musketry & Platoon Drill - Inspection at 2M. by OAE, GOE, Lt Col Grogan, D.S.O. left - Major T.R. Pardoe, D.S.O., Worcesters arrived & took over command - first operation orders	WA

WAR DIARY
or
INTELLIGENCE SUMMARY.

Army Form C. 2118.

Place	Date	Hour	Summary of Events and Information	Remarks and references to Appendices
Le Paradis	19/6/18		Made out - 6 Officers & 6 N.C.O.'s from Companies inspected Trenches - C.T. Instructor from Brigade for tomorrow.	W.D
"	20/6/18		Training by Companies (March discipline, fire Drill, Handling of Arms, Musketry & Platoon Drill) - All officers seen & addressed by Brig. Genl. at 1.45 P.M. - 2/Lt Graham joined for duty - 2/Lt Plews & 1 O.R. went on leave.	W.D
"	21/6/18		Training by Companies (Kinds of discipline for Drill Squad & Platoon Drill & Musketry) in forenoon - at 2 P.M. C.O.'s Muster Parade - at 5 P.M. Lecture to Officers by Brig. Genl. - Examination of Rifles by Expert Armourers & defective ones exchanged - Conference with Company Commanders - Major Wallis, H.F. Wiltshires, joined as Second in Command.	W.D

WAR DIARY
or
INTELLIGENCE SUMMARY.

(Erase heading not required.)

Army Form C. 2118.

Place	Date	Hour	Summary of Events and Information	Remarks and references to Appendices
LaParais	22/6/18		Battalion paraded at Nieurlet, & took part in Brigade Route march - Special precautions taken against men falling out on march without sufficient cause - Major Pardoe left & Major Wallis took over command.	
Staples area U10C26&27	23/6/18		Battalion moved at 10 A.M. to St Omer. Entrained there at 12.30 P.M. & proceeded to Staples area - erected tents & bivouacs & laid out camp - D Company temporarily accommodated in billets - Battalion H.Q. at U10C26 Sheet 27	
"	24/6/18		In forenoon M.O.'s inspection of Battalion - inspection of rifles & equipment by Companies - general cleaning up of camp & camouflage of tents & bivouacs - in afternoon inspection by Inspector of Medical Services - orders issued for special precautions in use of water - Lt Col Tew, H.S., C.M.G., East Surrey Regt arrived & took over command - Gay Parade.	

WAR DIARY
or
INTELLIGENCE SUMMARY.

Army Form C. 2118.

Place	Date	Hour	Summary of Events and Information	Remarks and references to Appendices
Staple Aux	25/6/18		Muster Roll parade & inspection by C.O. in forenoon — Special orders issued as to Box Respirators & Steel Helmets — Camp Standard Orders issued — Battalion marched in fighting kit with Lewis Guns to vicinity of Trenches at Q31 Central where Battalion was halted — C.O. took all Officers to the position in the trenches assigned to Battalion at V9 Central and pointed out the probable duties required in the event of the Trenches being manned.	
"	26/6/18		Battalion inspected by C.O. in the forenoon — after inspection drill under Company arrangements — D Company left billets & came into Camp — Water dump formed at Q31 Central. Ammunition dump at V15 a 51 — Conference with Company Commanders — H.8 boy went to Baths — Capt Reeve Smith transferred to A Company — Lieut L.C. Bertram to command C Coy.	

WAR DIARY
or
INTELLIGENCE SUMMARY.
(Erase heading not required.)

Army Form C. 2118.

Place	Date	Hour	Summary of Events and Information	Remarks and references to Appendices
Staple Inne	27/6/18	A.M. 8.30	A, B, & D Coys paraded for G.O.C.'s inspection & thereafter to both to Coy for inspection of Box Respirators & thereafter to the range at U.12.d.74.5h.27 for shooting & musketry - C Coy had Box Respirators inspected - Remainder of Company Commanders - P.T. Instructors from Brigade for whole day.	
"	28/6/18		A & B Coys went to the range for musketry & were visited by Brig. Gen. & G.O. - 44 G.R. of Battalion less than B1. were sent to Labour Corps Base - C & D drilled under Company arrangements - Transport Party returned with additional transport - Capt Burker left for C.C.S. sick	
"	29/6/18	A.M 8.30	Battalion in Marc for G.O.C.'s inspection. B Coy (4 off & 120 O.R) proceeded to range U.12.d.74.5h.27 to commence building a range	

WAR DIARY
or
INTELLIGENCE SUMMARY.
(Erase heading not required.)

Army Form C. 2118.

Place	Date	Hour	Summary of Events and Information	Remarks and references to Appendices
Staple Inn	29/6/18		under R.E. Officer — Remainder of Batt. (less Specialists) at disposal of Coy Officers (for Mark drill, musketry, saluting, handling of arms &c.	
		(M) 12.30	M.O.'s inspection of Battalion (less B Coy) without tunics & with shirts open for examination of skin — 2 cases found of skin disease — team furnace first first aid course	
		2	Companies at disposal of Coy Officers for drill &c Visited 107 Brigade in funeral Captain fielding left and Capt Fisher joined for duty as M.O.	+++
	30/6/18	A.M. 8.30	B & D Coys went to range for musketry — A & 3 Platoons of C Coys went to the range to complete Sand — Time other than at range occupied in drill under Company arrange-	
		11.30	-ments — Pay Parades — C.O. visited Brig. Genl. — Major Wallis left	+1

W. S. New Lt. Col.
Cmdg 12th Jan. Bn. N. Staff. R.
30/6/18

Vol 2

Confidential

War Diary

1/2th. Batn. North Stafford Regt.

From July 1st 1918 to July 31st 1918

(Volume III.)

Army Form C. 2118.

WAR DIARY
INTELLIGENCE SUMMARY.
(Erase heading not required.)

Instructions regarding War Diaries and Intelligence Summaries are contained in F. S. Regs., Part II. and the Staff Manual respectively. Title pages will be prepared in manuscript.

Place	Date	Hour	Summary of Events and Information	Remarks and references to Appendices.
Staple	1/7/18	A.M. 8.30	Battalion paraded (with Lewis Gunners & S/B) for C.O.'s inspection	
		9.30	Coys at disposal of Company Commanders for P.T., Arms Drill & Musketry	
		2-3 PM	Musketry	
		P.M.	Recruit Platoons at range firing	
		3.15"	Conference with Company Commanders	
		5-45"	Lecture to Senior Officers by Corps Gas Officer	
"	2/7/18	A.M. 8.30	C.O.'s parade – Inspection by C.O. & detailed instruction for afternoon employment	
		10.30	Coys at disposal of Coy Cmdrs for further instruction in firing equipment	
		12 P.M.		
		2	Battalion paraded & marched to Bgde parade ground	
		3	Inspection by H.R.H. The Duke of Connaught	
		7.15	Conference of Company Cmdrs	
	3/7/18	AM 7	All Coys at range firing – Range available only between 12 & 1	
			G.M. Owing to another Brigade using it – Musketry exercise	

Army Form C. 2118.

WAR DIARY
or
INTELLIGENCE SUMMARY.
(Erase heading not required.)

Instructions regarding War Diaries and Intelligence Summaries are contained in F. S. Regs., Part II. and the Staff Manual respectively. Title pages will be prepared in manuscript.

Place	Date	Hour	Summary of Events and Information	Remarks and references to Appendices
Staple	3/7/18	P.M. 1.15	Whole working turn at the range — C & D Coies (less Recruits)	
		3.15	Supplying working parties at range	
			Conference of Coy Cmdrs — Sergt Instructor of Musketry for Bttn appointed.	
"	4/7/18	A.M. 6.45	A & B Coies at work on the range	
		7	C & D Coies saluting drill	
		6.45	C & D Coies at distance of Coy Officers for Musketry, tric sines	Apdx
		12-5	— rline, judging distance ra	
		1	A & B Coies firing at range, C & D at 3 P.M.	
		2.30	Visited by Brig. Genl	
"	5/7/18	A.M. 7	A & B Coies saluting drill	
		7.45	C & D at range firing —	
		8.45	A & B — P.T. & B.T., squad drill & rifle exercises — Various detailed —	
			range forming digging parties — 2 O.M. Company drill & particular range	

A6945 Wt. W14421/M1160 350,000 12/16 D. D. & L. Forms/C./2118/14.

Army Form C. 2118.

WAR DIARY
or
INTELLIGENCE SUMMARY.
(Erase heading not required.)

Instructions regarding War Diaries and Intelligence Summaries are contained in F.S. Regs., Part II. and the Staff Manual respectively. Title pages will be prepared in manuscript.

Place	Date	Hour	Summary of Events and Information	Remarks and references to Appendices
Staple	6/7/18	A.M. 7	All Coys at range firing	
		8	A & B Coys at Baths	
		P.M. 3	Lewis gunners at range firing 7 casuals of A & B Coys	
"	7/7/18	A.M. 8-12	C & D Coys at range firing	
		P.M. 12-4	A & B Coys at range firing – work parties at range – Barbers for Coys appointed – 2/Lt Stafford appointed Adjutant	M
"	8/7/18	AM PM 8-4	All Coys at range firing – parties both with and without Box Respirators – Bad shots fired again by themselves when not firing Coys at boy drill, PT & BT r – 2/Lt Parkinson appointed Battn Gas Officer.	
"	9/7/18	A.M. 9	Battn Parade – Inspection of transport – Specialists (say L.G & SB) Receive special instruction – Bad shots instructed in Musketry Subaltern Officers Squad drill – NCO's instruction in B.T. & P.T.	

Army Form C. 2118.

WAR DIARY
or
INTELLIGENCE SUMMARY.
(Erase heading not required.)

Place	Date	Hour	Summary of Events and Information	Remarks and references to Appendices
Staple	10/7/18	A.M. 6:45	C & D Coys at range. C & D Coy working at range	
		8	B & D Coys at Truths — A & D Coys at range firing	
		P.M. 12:45	B Coy working at range — A & D Coys extended order drill — all available NCOs at PT & BT instruction — Subalterns Officers instructed by Lac Officer — C & D Coy Commanders inspecting trenches	C.O.
Hazebrouck	11/7/18	A.M. 9	Battn proceeded to occupy E. Hazebrouck line — Relieved 13th East Lancs at noon — 2 Coys in support line & line of Resistance & 2 Coys in support — Patrols sent out — T dulies carried out as of in front line system — Enemy aircraft at night — some bombs dropped — also enemy counter artillery shelling	
"	12/7/18		Trench Warfare routine — Outposts & pickets visited frequently & instructed in duties — Special attention to field of fire from	

WAR DIARY
INTELLIGENCE SUMMARY.
(Erase heading not required.)

Army Form C. 2118.

Instructions regarding War Diaries and Intelligence Summaries are contained in F. S. Regs., Part II. and the Staff Manual respectively. Title pages will be prepared in manuscript.

Place	Date	Hour	Summary of Events and Information	Remarks and references to Appendices
Hazebrouck	13/7/18		Trek — improvements carried out on L.G. positions — trench digging — counter artillery shelling — enemy aircraft activity at night — some bombs dropped — work parties supplied to R.E.	
"	14/7/18		Trench warfare routine continued — dries in supply relieved — Coys in Picket & Outpost lines — workparties supplied to R.E.	
"			Trench warfare routine continued — work parties supplied to R.E. — Counter artillery shelling — some enemy aircraft activity at night.	WM
Staple	15/7/18	7.25 A.M.	Battn moved out of E. Hazebrouck line back to Camp at Staple — 400 yards between Coys — kept 15 established & inspection of rear of men under Coy arrangements	
"	16.7.18	8.30	All Coys (excluding Specialists) had Church Parade — aran	

A6945 Wt. W1422/M1160 350,000 12/16 D.D. & L. Forms/C/2118/14.

WAR DIARY
or
INTELLIGENCE SUMMARY.
(Erase heading not required.)

Army Form C. 2118.

Place	Date	Hour	Summary of Events and Information	Remarks and references to Appendices
Hazybrouck	17-7-18	A.M. 11	Met at Jas Chaurier Series at disposal of Coy Commanders for the discipline & company Drill P.T. & B.T. — Subaltern Officers aypred drill — NCO's at P.T. & B.T. instruction. Battalion proceeded to Hazebrouck and were billeted by Coys — Coys at disposal of Coy Commanders for fatigues &c	O.M.
"	18/7/18	A.M. 7-8	NCO's PT & BT —	
		9-15	Coys at disposal of Coy Commanders for Coy drill PT & BT	
		12-45	Lewis Gunner under L.G. Officer & Stretcher bearers under M.O.	
		6.30	Battalion moved to Borre into support line.	

WAR DIARY
INTELLIGENCE SUMMARY.
(Erase heading not required.)

Army Form C. 2118.

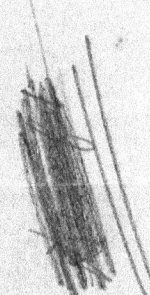

Place	Date	Hour	Summary of Events and Information	Remarks and references to Appendices
Borre	19/7/18		Battalion continued in ~~reserve~~ ~~support~~ — Various work parties detailed to R.E.'s for trench digging, revetting &c — Training under Company arrangements so far as work parties permitted permitted. — Visits to support line.	
"	20/7/18		Battalion still in reserve — Various work parties as before to R.E.'s — Training under Coy arrangements practically Nil owing to men being on working parties	
"	21/7/18		As yesterday	
Buysse House	22/7/18		Battalion relieved 13th K.S. Lanc in support at 10 p.m. Bn. H.Q. Buysse House E 3 c 1.8. All available men on night Working Parties.	

WAR DIARY
or
INTELLIGENCE SUMMARY.
(Erase heading not required.)

Army Form C. 2118.

Place	Date	Hour	Summary of Events and Information	Remarks and references to Appendices
Canal du Nord	23/7/18		Battalion continues in support. Working parties supplied as before	
"	24/7		do	
"	25/7		do	
			Reconnaissance of front line as appd. by Coy Cdrs.	all
ST BAZEEL STATION	26/7		At night Batt relieved 13th E. Lancs in front line. Dispositions — Left front Coy D. Right front Coy B. Close support A Coy. Support C Coy. Bn H.Q. E.11.a.O.9. Our front runs E.12.b.4.4. E.12 Cent E.12.c.0.6. E.11.d.6.3. E.11.a.3.2. Posts of above Platoon strength with intervals of from 70 to 200 yds between.	
	27/7		Battn continues in front line. Casualties 1 K 4 W	

A6945 Wt. W14422/M1160 350,000 12/16 D.D. & L. Forms/C/2118/14.

Army Form C. 2118.

WAR DIARY
INTELLIGENCE SUMMARY.
(Erase heading not required.)

Place	Date	Hour	Summary of Events and Information	Remarks and references to Appendices
STRAZEELE STATION	28/7		Battalion continued in front line. 1 German Corporal taken prisoner.	
	29/7		Battalion continued in front line.	
	30/7	12.15 am	Battalion continued in front line. Enemy attacked MERRIS Switchover on our right. This caused heavy shelling of our village all day with HE and Gas. At night our patrols captured a German patrol of 1 Ops + 2 O.R.	nil
	31/7		Battn relieved at night by 2 3/9 Cheshires + moved down into Reserve line at BOR RE.	

Lt-Col
Comdg 1/6th
St. Staffs Regt

WO 3

Confidential

War Diary.

12th. Batn. North. Stafford. Regt.

From 1st August 1918 to 31st August 1918.

(Volume III).

Army Form C. 2118.

WAR DIARY
or
INTELLIGENCE SUMMARY.
(Erase heading not required.)

Instructions regarding War Diaries and Intelligence Summaries are contained in F. S. Regs., Part II. and the Staff Manual respectively. Title pages will be prepared in manuscript.

Place	Date	Hour	Summary of Events and Information	Remarks and references to Appendices
BORRE	1/8		Batt. in reserve relieved by 8th Royal Irish event of 1/8 and marched back to Camp at STAPLE	
STAPLE	2/8		A & B Coys Bathing & changing underclothes	
"	3/8		C & D Coys Bathing & changing underclothes All Coys out inspection	OK
"	4/8		Brigade Church Parade on field near Bn HQ at 11am	
"	5/8		B & C Coys Gas to Range firing B & D Bath & Lewis Gun at Range	

Army Form C. 2118.

WAR DIARY
or
INTELLIGENCE SUMMARY.
(Erase heading not required.)

Instructions regarding War Diaries and Intelligence Summaries are contained in F. S. Regs., Part II. and the Staff Manual respectively. Title pages will be prepared in manuscript.

Place	Date 1918	Hour	Summary of Events and Information	Remarks and references to Appendices
Staples	6/8/		"B" & "D" Coy. Baths & Range firing. A.C. "C" Coy. Range firing.	
"	7/8		All Coys doing P. Training, Bayonet fighting, Entrance Course "C" & "D" Coy. Range.	
"	8/8		All Coys. Entrenching, Gass & Entrance exam, Physical Training, Bayonet fighting.	Ord
"	9/8		All Coys - P. Training - Bayonet fighting - Musketry instruction "A" & "D" Coys on Range.	
"	10/8		Divine Service - C/E's in Chateau field - R.C. Church at Etaples - Musketry parade from 13th Scottish.	
"	11/8		Regimental Sports.	

Army Form C. 2118.

WAR DIARY
or
~~INTELLIGENCE SUMMARY.~~
(Erase heading not required.)

Instructions regarding War Diaries and Intelligence Summaries are contained in F. S. Regs., Part II. and the Staff Manual respectively. Title pages will be prepared in manuscript.

Place	Date	Hour	Summary of Events and Information	Remarks and references to Appendices
STAPLE	12/8		All Ordnance or Range General Training - Bomb throw from "B" Company under 231st Field Coy for instructions	
	13/8		All Coys at Baths. All Coys ordinary general training	
	14/8		All Coys at Baths - "A" & "C" Coys night operations 9-11pm	Nil
	15/8		General Training. Relieve Officers at lecture "How to read Aerial Photographs". Line Officers at Sanitary Lecture at K.Ovo. H.Q Sanitary Sec.	
	16/8		8.30am Battalion parade for tactical exercise in neighbourhood of RYVEL HOUT CASTEEL. "A" & "B" Coys with "C" & "D" in support attacked a flagged enemy under Major Pearson	
	17/8		Brigade Sports	

WAR DIARY
INTELLIGENCE SUMMARY

Army Form C. 2118.

Place	Date	Hour	Summary of Events and Information	Remarks and references to Appendices
STAPLE	18/8		Brunt Service. COFS in Chateau field. H.Q at STAPLE. Men and horses accommodated 13 East Raines.	
"	19/8		Arrival Horseshow - horses entered from each Company to the shows. "B" + "C" Coys on Range. "A" + "D" Coys general training	
"	20/8		Battn took part in Brigade Tactical Exercise being in support to 13" R. Irwin Fus who attacked the enemy (13" East Raines)	[signature]
"	21/8		All Coys B.T. + L.B Training, Musketry, patrolling flag drill. "B" + "C" Coys night operations 9.30 - 11 p.m. "A" + "D" Coys on Range.	

WAR DIARY
or
INTELLIGENCE SUMMARY.
(Erase heading not required.)

Army Form C. 2118.

Place	Date	Hour	Summary of Events and Information	Remarks and references to Appendices
	22/8		The Batt. moved into the line & took over from the 12th Norfolks and York & Lancasters that Bn. The Reserve line was taken up by the Battln. were (less 1 Sec. M.G.) from E.10.a.48.46 Colley Cottages E.21.a and "D" Coy advanced at E.17.6.55.	
	23/8		Holding same line. "D" Coy relieved men every M.G. rome L.G. "C" & "D" Coy having moving in covering parties for East of Ames Regt into bed the Front line.	OHL.
	24/8		Holding same line. "A" Coy relieved D Coy in their forward position.	

WAR DIARY
or
INTELLIGENCE SUMMARY.
(Erase heading not required.)

Army Form C. 2118.

Place	Date	Hour	Summary of Events and Information	Remarks and references to Appendices
	25/6		Cottages at Colley Cottages of G.O.C. Brigade of the Div and O/C Battalion	
			On the night of 25/26/6/18 we took over the front line from the 13t East Lancs Batt.	
			Br.C. Coy on the front line	
			D " Support	
			A " (Rear) reserve	
			The general held were :- (Sheet 36a.N.E)	
			C. Coy bell front Coy from F21a.55 to F21c.24	
			B " right " " " F21C.24 " F27a.77	
			D " in support " F20c.75	
			A " reserve " F13c.32 " F19a.48	

Army Form C. 2118.

WAR DIARY
or
INTELLIGENCE SUMMARY.
(Erase heading not required.)

Place	Date	Hour	Summary of Events and Information	Remarks and references to Appendices
	26/8		One previous shelter by "C" Coy showed sent to Ypres. B & C Coy carried out active patrolling during the night.	
	27/8	10 am	One afternoon was carried out by the 13th Canadians (Batt. on our right) which was quite successful. One platoon of A Coy 13th Bath was made be duty during the operation to the Lewis riding. At 12.30 p.m. the remaining two platoons of A Coy were ordered to report to Lieut. Col. Rath for duty during the operation. "B" Coy and night front Coy continued & kept in touch with the Canadians during the attack. Consolidated position our trench such that Batt. advanced Batt. H. Q. forward at F.20.c.7.5	
	28/8		1 platoon of D Coy was sent up to support B Coy on right front.	

WAR DIARY
or
INTELLIGENCE SUMMARY

Army Form C. 2118.

Place	Date	Hour	Summary of Events and Information	Remarks and references to Appendices
	29/8		"D" Coy returned to their original line from the 13th Canterbury. They were under the orders of the 13th North Staffs.	
	30/8		According to orders active patrols were sent out by our two forward Coys B & C to try & get in touch with the enemy. After pushing forward some distance 170 yds, no enemy troops or M.G. or Snipers were encountered. The Battalion advanced and occupied the yellow dotted line moving little except the Batt. H.Q. Losses 1 at 4-0 p.m. The Batt. took up the line except the Coys were lying on F 16 d 14 & the right on F 28 c 33. The ground was taken without opposition. 3 killed 1 died of wounds, 33 wounded 3 missing.	

WAR DIARY
or
INTELLIGENCE SUMMARY.

(Erase heading not required.)

Army Form C. 2118.

Place	Date	Hour	Summary of Events and Information	Remarks and references to Appendices
	3/8	1·am	The 2 sub Cheshire Regt took over the line of our Lines Honorable Corps - B + C. The 23rd Lancashire Fusiliers had arrived Reserve positions held respectively by D + A Coys.	
			Signed L Col Comdg 12 Nnorth Staffs Regt	

Army Form C. 2118.

119/1140
2/N Stafford

2/SR 4

WAR DIARY
or
INTELLIGENCE SUMMARY.

(Erase heading not required.)

Instructions regarding War Diaries and Intelligence Summaries are contained in F. S. Regs., Part II. and the Staff Manual respectively. Title pages will be prepared in manuscript.

Place	Date	Hour	Summary of Events and Information	Remarks and references to Appendices
Sheet 36A NE. SWARTENBROCK	1/9		Battalion in Reserve line forming nucleus garrison	
			Dispositions:- Batt. Hq. E.14.d.5.3.	
			A Coy K.4.a.6.0. to E.21.d.0.0	
			B Coy E.21.d.0.0 to E.15 Cent.	
			C Coy E.15 cent. to E.10.a.6.7	
			D Coy E.14.d.	
"	2/9		B and C Coys attached to 17th (P) Bn Worc. Regt. for road work in vicinity of LABIS FARM	call
"	3/9		A & D Coy and Bn Hq batting ar Dive Baths D.18.c.8.3.	
PONT WEMEAU	4/9		Batt. Hq. A and D Coys advance to Farm at 7.23.c.40.	
"	5/9		B and C Coys join the Batt. at 7.23.c.40.	

Army Form C. 2118.

WAR DIARY
or
INTELLIGENCE SUMMARY.
(Erase heading not required.)

Instructions regarding War Diaries and Intelligence Summaries are contained in F. S. Regs., Part II. and the Staff Manual respectively. Title pages will be prepared in manuscript.

Place	Date	Hour	Summary of Events and Information	Remarks and references to Appendices
STEENWERK SWITCH	6/9		Batt. moves up into STEENWERK SWITCH in Brigade Reserve (Sheet 36 NW) occupying the trench from A23a07 to G4d88. Disposition. Coys from Left to Right - B.D.C.A. Battn Hq. A28 b7.3. Transport Lines at Vintage Farm A22 b9.6.	
NIPPON BEND	7/9		Battalion moves up in support in vicinity of TANDY FM. Battn Hq. at - 36B 1962.4.	call
NIEPPE SYSTEM	8/9		Battalion moves up into front line relieving 13th Bn E Lanco Regt in advance square. Bn HQ at POSTON FM B20 c42. Companies occupying NIEPPE SYSTEM. D Coy B16 d 9.0 to B22 d 3.3 C Coy B22 d 3.3 to B26 d 67 A Coy B26 d 4.0 to B28 d 2.4 B Coy in support at B 21 d 7.8.	

WAR DIARY
INTELLIGENCE SUMMARY.
(Erase heading not required.)

Army Form C. 2118.

Place	Date	Hour	Summary of Events and Information	Remarks and references to Appendices
Pont de NIEPPE	9/9		Post stationed at MANCHESTER KEEP by C Coy. Continuous patrolling into and around village of PONT du NIEPPE.	
"	10/9 and 11/9 Night 11/9 - 12/9		Active patrolling by day and night on the whole front. Under cover of darkness our left flank moved forward though PONT du NIEPPE village to line B17c0.7 B17a5.1 B17d4.3 B23b8.6 B23d.99 B23d.97 MANCHESTER KEEP B28b8.4 Bridgehead at B23 & 96.70 was seized Coy A in PONT de NIEPPE left to right D.B.C. Support coy A Village in reserve.	NULL OPERATION ORDER ATTACHED
"	12/9		Scoring Patrols were pushed forward. An enemy attempt to recapture the village was driven off.	

WAR DIARY
INTELLIGENCE SUMMARY
(Erase heading not required.)

Army Form C. 2118.

Place	Date	Hour	Summary of Events and Information	Remarks and references to Appendices
PONT DE NIEPPE	12/9 contd.		Our posts although subjected to continuous harassing fire maintained their positions.	
"	Night 12/9 13/9		We occupied the farm at B.17d 05 80 (D Coy) and established a post at B.17d 0.9. A patrol intending to cross the river Lys at B 23d 90 75 - found the river in flood and he bridges destroyed. It was consequently unable to carry out our intended operations on the eastern bank.	
GRAND BEAUMART	13/9		Our posts maintained their positions. At night the Brigade was relieved by 120 Infy Bde and marched our 16 killers at - GRAND BEAUMART Battn HQ Farm A16a 6.2. Total casualties this tour:- Off. 2 W. OR. 15 K 35 W 13 M.	

Army Form C. 2118.

WAR DIARY
INTELLIGENCE SUMMARY
(Erase heading not required.)

Place	Date	Hour	Summary of Events and Information	Remarks and references to Appendices
GRAND BEAUMART	14/9		Men resting & cleaning up. Cluts recoverve.	
"	15/9		Parades under coy arrangements for completion of outfitting &c.	
"	16/9		Battalion inspection by Commdg Officer	
"	17/9		Batt. on Brigade inspection by B.O.C. 119 Brigade	
"	18/9		Batt. on Brigade inspection by B.O.C. 40 Divn. Preparation of May Madame arrangements	
"	19/9		See coys parade under coy arrangements for outlee & bit inspection	

Army Form C. 2118.

WAR DIARY
or
INTELLIGENCE SUMMARY.
(Erase heading not required.)

Place	Date	Hour	Summary of Events and Information	Remarks and references to Appendices
GRAND BEQUARD	20/9		All Coys provide working parties for repair of main road in vicinity of Tiger Farm.	
HAZEBROUCK	21/9		Batt. moved back (with rest of Brigade) into reserve at HAZEBROUCK. Bn H.Q. at Institution Jeanne D'Arc Rue d'Aire. Bn entrained at BAILLEUL 1130 a.m.	Sketch 3 ⊕ 18 c 8.3.
"	22/9		All coys lecturing etc. Divine Service 11 am Church Parade.	
	23/9		Batt. prepared to move forward, arrangements being made to leave HAZEBROUCK by train for BAILLEUL at 11am. when Batt. arrived at HAZEBROUCK 515 new arrangements were cancelled and Batt. returned to billets	

WAR DIARY
INTELLIGENCE SUMMARY

Army Form C. 2118.

Sheet 36 N.W.

Place	Date	Hour	Summary of Events and Information	Remarks and references to Appendices
HAZEBROUCK	24/9		Battalion inspected by Commanding Officer in morning. Afternoon spent in training in Lewis Gun Bombing.	
"	25/9		Battalion inspected by G.O.C. 119th Brigade in morning. Afternoon spent in training in Lewis Gun & Bombing.	
"	26/9		Battalion entrained at HAZEBROUCK Station at 11 a.m. for BAILLEUL, then marched to reserve position of front line dispositions. "A" Coy B7 b 8 1. "C" Coy B7 d 5.7. "B" Coy B7 d 7.7. "D" Coy B8 a.a.2. (Sheet 36 NW) B.H.Q. B7 d 9.2.	
MEUNIERS	27/9 28/9		Interior Economy. Training in Lewis Guns. Whole Battalion engaged in Lewis Gun training. Two companies received treatment to feet at Foot Centre.	
"	29/9		Whole Battalion training firing Lewis Guns. Remainder of Battn. received treatment to feet. Draft of 1 Officer + 77 O/R joined for duty.	
NIEPPE	30/9		Battalion moved to NIEPPE system in support. Dispositions: B.H.Q. B10 b 3.1 "A" Coy B11 C 1.3 "D" B11 C 1.9	

Army Form C. 2118.

WAR DIARY
or
INTELLIGENCE SUMMARY.
(Erase heading not required.)

Place	Date	Hour	Summary of Events and Information	Remarks and references to Appendices
NIEPPE SHEET 36.N.W.	31/9 cont.		B. Coy B10 a 95.75 to B 4 d 35.30. C " B16 d 98 to B11 c 1.4 D " B11 a 1.0 to B10 b 7.8 Immediately after arrival at position A Coy were sent forward to OOSTHOVE FARM B11 d Central. (36 NW) to await advance of R Bris two when they were to move forward form a defensive flank on the right. They moved off to carry this out at 02.00 4/10/18 took up position B18 Central to O13 c4.7. in touch with Cheshires on the right & R Irish on left	Cas.

W. Whillans?
Lt Col.
Commanding
12th North'd Fus Regt.

1/10/18

Army Form C. 2118.

INTELLIGENCE SUMMARY
WAR DIARY
or
(Erase heading not required.)
Summary of Events and Information

Place	Date	Hour		

Instructions regarding War Diaries and Intelligence Summaries are contained in F.S. Regs., Part II. and the Staff Manual respectively. Title pages will be prepared in manuscript.

Bde

J.1720. W.W.V.&L. Ltd. D.D/P.51. 350000. 11/16. N.M.W.

Operation Order No 9   Copy No.
by 12 Bn. X Staff Regt.   B

Map Sheet 36 NW
1/10000

1. Tonight 1/5" By will advance their
   Line as follows.
2. "A" Coy in present positions until
   relieved by a Coy of the R.W.N.S
   Fus when they will move to
   the line B23 d 2.8 to B23 b 6.4.
   B Coy   B23 d 9.8 - B23 b 3.1
           B 17 a 2 4
   C Coy & B28 b 8 4 MANCHESTER
   KEEP   B23 d 9 8.
   D Coy   B17 d 24 - B17 c 7.7 -
           B 17 c 4 0

3. D Coy will send a strong
   Patrol of 1 Platoon under an
   Officer to gain Line of the Road
   B18 a 1.7 to B18 a 6.8 and a
   second patrol under an Officer
   to gain the Line B18 a 1.9 to
   B 18 a 6 3 ½
   Tomorrow morning Operations
   will be undertaken to establish
   Strong points on Y line B 24 b 6.9
   and B 24 b 4.8

Six men per platoon will carry
4 Rifle Grenades each and every
man will carry two bombs.

7. The signal for new line being
reached & the Bridgehead positions
being established will be 2
White Very Lights fired in quick
succession.

8. Watches will be synchronised
at Advanced BHQ at 4.0am
an Officer per Coy will report at
that hour.

9. Contact Planes will call for
Flares at 7.0am & 7.30am when
all advanced troops will
light flares & show discs.
Every other man will carry a red
flare. Red Flares will be lit
whenever called for by Contact
Planes.

10. M Guns will take up positions
as follows by 4.0am
1 Gun at MANCHESTER KEEP
2 Guns in NIEPPE SYSTEM at 16a85

4(cont'd) At 5/10am a heavy bombardment will be opened on the JUTE FACTORY, the house about B29 b.9.9 & the house at B24 c.2.7 The road embankment from PONT de NIEPPE will also be searched at 5.10am. Two platoons of "C" Coy will rush the Bridge at B29 b.6.9 and establish themselves about houses B29.b.9.9 and will send a patrol of One Officer 10 OR to reconnoitre the JUTE FACTORY.

The remaining two platoons of "C" Coy will move forward in close support about B29 b.2.8. to B23.d.4.2. These two platoons will be ready to cross bridge to support leading platoons.

B Coy will rush Bridge at B24 c.0.8 & establish themselves about houses at B24 c.2.7.

"A" Coy will send a platoon to take over the posts vacated by "B" Coy at B23 d.9.8. & be ready to move across Bridge.

5. Two Stokes Guns will be moved to positions at B23 d.5.2 & 2 guns at B23 b.8.3.

CONFIDENTIAL

WAR DIARY

12th Battn. North Staffs Regt.

VOL. 5

FROM 1-10-18.
TO 31-10-18.

Army Form C. 2118.

WAR DIARY
INTELLIGENCE SUMMARY.
(Erase heading not required.)

Place	Date	Hour	Summary of Events and Information	Remarks and references to Appendices
NIEPPE	1918 1/10		Battalion in support with two Companies forward. A Coy holding defensive flank and B Coy taking over portion of front line on the R. Lwo. Dispositions:- A Coy B 18 Cent- to E 13 c 4.7 forward. D Coy C.13 c. 38 to C 7 c 4.4 (Sheet 36).	Ylal 6
"	2/10		Battalion engaged in strengthening and improving trenches. A and B Coys withdrawn from forward positions at nightfall, as owing to advance of R. Inns. Fus. they were no longer necessary.	
HOUPLINES	3/10		Battalion took over from line position in old British Trench system. Dispositions:- B.H.Q. C 22 c 75.35. A Coy C 22 c 75.25 to C 28 a 8.8 D Coy C 22 a 75.50 to C 22 b 88.50 C Coy C 28 b to C 29 a D Coy I 4 a 5.8 to I 3 d 4.2.	
"	4/10		Nine prisoners taken from capture ground on mopping up. At 18.00 hrs C Coy working from London Rd Trench C 28 d 8.7 proceeded down old	

Army Form C. 2118.

WAR DIARY
INTELLIGENCE SUMMARY.
(Erase heading not required.)

Place	Date	Hour	Summary of Events and Information	Remarks and references to Appendices
HOUPLINES	1918 4/10 Contd		ced British front line trench. It was found clear of enemy and posts were established at I.5.c.7.8 and I.5.c.3.3. An attempt was forced down to railway was forced by enemy M.G. down to I.10.b.5.7. D Coy then took up position in gap at I.29.a and captured farm I.10.b.6.7. B Coy Centre in I.29.a and farm line was pushed out posts in C.23.c finely established down whole length from C.23.c to I.5.c.3.9. with post in farm I.10.b.5.7. line I.5.c.2.0 – I.11.a.5.0. Enemy reported in line I.5.c.8.9.	
"	5/10		An attempt to enter enemy front line system failed. Enemy appeared to expect attack and met us with strong M.G. fire, trench system being strongly manned by infantry. We retaliated to left, but withdrew later owing to failure of centre and right. Post withdrawn from farm I.10.b.5.7. at 2.3.5 – 9. No enemy barrage put down on support trench in C.28.d.	

WAR DIARY
INTELLIGENCE SUMMARY.
(Erase heading not required.)

Army Form C. 2118.

Place	Date	Hour	Summary of Events and Information	Remarks and references to Appendices
HOUPLINES	1918 6/10		Posn again established in farm I 10 d 5.7 and touch gained with 120 Infy Bde on our right. Small posn in C 23 a 1.6 raided by enemy - garrison apparently captured. Posn at I 10 b 5.7 pushed forward to I 10 d 9.7.	
"	7/10.		Line withdrawn to connected trench system with right resting on railway at I 10 d 9.7 running N to I 5 c 2.7 thence down Fre. Rd. to C 28 c 5.2 then N 16 c 22 d 40.95. Battalion relieved by K.O.Y.L.I. (120 Bde) total casualties this tour:- Killed 1 off. 4 OR. Wounded 5 off. 26 OR. Wounded & missing 1 off. Missing 10 OR.	
	8/10		Battalion moved to C 20 d 35.75 from line and from on to H 3 a 5.3. Cleaning up & for inspection of draft by G.O.C.	
	9/10		Battn. inspected by C.O. Organisation of coys. checked. Training in I.g. & rifle exercises.	

WAR DIARY
or
INTELLIGENCE SUMMARY.

Place	Date	Hour	Summary of Events and Information	Remarks and references to Appendices
	12/9/18		M.M. inspected by C.O. & organisation checked N.E.PPE 5,15.M	
			recommences by A.i.Cm's.	
	11/10		Baths at North A.22. Training in Lg. Thinking	
	13/10		Batt. moved to GRAND BEAUMART. Dispositions	
			Bt.HQ, A + B Cnys A.16.C.6.2.	
			C A.16.d.1.7.	
			D A.16.e.10.95.	
	13/10/18		Relieved by 8º R. Irish Regt.	
			Church Parade and demonstration at 1000 hrs "field"	
			inspected by C.O.	
	14/10		Companies training in musketry and in	
			attack on machine gun posts.	
	15/10		C.O's inspection. Whole battalion passed through	
			Gas Chamber at STEENWERK.	

Army Form C. 2118.

WAR DIARY
or
INTELLIGENCE SUMMARY.
(Erase heading not required.)

Place	Date	Hour	Summary of Events and Information	Remarks and references to Appendices
	16/10		Attack scheme postponed on account of adverse weather. Singing competition for platoons at 14.00 hrs (singing on the march)	
	17/10		Battalion moved from GRAND BEAUMART to camp (wooden huts) at 36 B 19 a 3.4, one coy at B 20 a 0.9	
	18/10		Battalion moved to camp (German Huts) at 36 C 30 d 5.2	
	19/10		Battalion moved to camp (German huts) at 36 I 12 b 9.3. Battn. HQ at 36 J 7 c 0.9. Working party carrying out reconnaissance strength in officers and O.R. provided for work on ARMENTIERES—LILLE Rly in square 36 J 16 (12.00 hrs to 18.00 hrs inclusive of marching one hr each way)	
	20/10		Church parade cancelled. Companies training in morning as above. Working party again furnished to ARMENTIERES as above. 3 off and 100 O.R. proceeded to ARMENTIERES as Guard of Honour to French President on his visit on 21/10/18	

Place	Date	Hour	Summary of Events and Information	Remarks and references to Appendices
	21/10		Batt. attended Brigade parade at 9.0 hrs Presentation of medals by Divisional Commander. Working party again furnished as above	
	22/10		Battalion training the whole day and bathing in evening	
	23/10		Battalion continued to train — Musketry, Rifle Grenades & Lewis Gunnery. Singing competition in afternoon	
	24/10		Battalion marched to BONDUES and billeted in the village 36 E 23 b and E 24 a, carrying out advance guard scheme on the way	
	25/10		Battalion inspected by C.O. Cleaning up in afternoon	

Army Form C. 2118.

WAR DIARY
or
INTELLIGENCE SUMMARY.
(Erase heading not required.)

Place	Date	Hour	Summary of Events and Information	Remarks and references to Appendices
	26/10		Battalion left BONDUES for WATTRELOS marching through ROUBAIX. Billeted in Factory at 37A 14 d 0.5.	
	27/10		Church Parade in Cinema Hall, WATTRELOS Square	
	28/10		Training resumed — Musketry, P.T. + B.F. Close Order drill, Company in attack, Rifle grenades, smoke screen —	Roe
	29/10		Training continued	
	30/10		Training continued. Weekly singing competition. Demonstration by C Coy of the use of phosphorus bombs and No 36 Rifle grenades in the attack, attended by G.O.C.	
	31/10		Training continued.	

T. R. Bennet
LT-COLNL
COMMANDING 12TH
BK. N. STAFFS REGT.

CONFIDENTIAL.

9/8 6

12TH BN. NORTH STAFFORDS.

WAR DIARY.

Vol. VI

From :- 1/11/18.
To :- 30/11/18.

13"-

Army Form C. 2118.

WAR DIARY
or
INTELLIGENCE SUMMARY.
(Erase heading not required.)

Instructions regarding War Diaries and Intelligence Summaries are contained in F. S. Regs., Part II. and the Staff Manual respectively. Title pages will be prepared in manuscript.

Place	Date	Hour	Summary of Events and Information	Remarks and references to Appendices
	1918			
	1/11		Battalion moved forward from WATTRELOS to ESTAMPUIS	} N/S
	2/11		Training continued	
	3/11		Church Parade. Reconnaissance of front line by Bn HQ Officers and Coy Commanders.	
	4/11		Battalion left ESTAMPUIS and relieved 2/3rd Bn CHESHIRE Regt in front line (left sector of Divisional front) Relief completed at 21.30 hrs. Dispositions Map Sheet 37 Battn. H.Q. B 18 c 8.8 Two Support Coys Left C Coy C 13 a 4.9 Right B Coy B 24 d 4.9. Two forward Coys Left A Coy Coy HQ and 1 Plat. C 14 d 8.9 One platoon in two posts C 15 a 3.3 and C 15 a 5.5 Two platoons in four posts:- C 15 d 0.4, C 15 d 0.7 C 15 d 1.9 C 9 d 2.4	

WAR DIARY
INTELLIGENCE SUMMARY.
(Erase heading not required.)

Army Form C. 2118.

Place	Date	Hour	Summary of Events and Information	Remarks and references to Appendices
	4/11 contd.		Two forward Coys (contd). Right B Coy (in WARCOING Village) Coy H.Q. C 20 a. 8.4. One plat: C 20 a. 6.5. One plat. C 20 a. 8.3 One plat in three posts:- B 20 b 2.9 / B 20 b 7.7 / B 20 b 7.0. One plat in four posts:- B 20 c 9.8 / B 20 c 7.8 / B 20 c 5.9 / B 20 c 2.5	
	5/11		Dayeight patrols advancing from each coy front towards HERINNES encountered heavy M.G. fire and established the fact that the village was strongly held with from 15 to 20 M.G's. Enemy barrage put down on our lines in response to green light signals from enemy front line. At dusk D Coy relieved B Coy on right coy sector.	

Army Form C. 2118.

WAR DIARY
or
INTELLIGENCE SUMMARY.
(Erase heading not required.)

Instructions regarding War Diaries and Intelligence Summaries are contained in F.S. Regs., Part II. and the Staff Manual respectively. Title pages will be prepared in manuscript.

Place	Date	Hour	Summary of Events and Information	Remarks and references to Appendices
	6/11		Right Coy. front taken over by 14th Division as far as C.15.c.7.3. On the night we took over from 13th Bn E. Lancs. Regt. as far as C.26.a.4.0. Dispositions of Battn. now as Follows:- Battn. H.Q. B.24.d.4.9 Reserve Coy. A Coy. B.23.b.9.9 Support Coy. B Coy. C.19.c.3.3 Rear Support Coy. C Coy. C.20.a.0.4 Forward Coy. D Coy. Coy H.Q. C.20.a.9.4 One Plat - C.20.a.9.3 Three Platoons in Posts:- Right Plat- H.Q. C.20.b.4.7 Posts: C.25.c.8.6 Centre Plat- H.Q. C.20.c.8.8. Posts:- C.20.c.6.4 C.20.d.2.8 C.20.b.7.0 Left Plat- H.Q. C.20.b.4.3. Posts:- C.20.b.6.6 C.20.b.2.9	Obs.

WAR DIARY
OF
INTELLIGENCE SUMMARY.
(Erase heading not required.)

Army Form C. 2118.

Place	Date	Hour	Summary of Events and Information	Remarks and references to Appendices
	7/11		C Company relieved D Coy. in front line. Bridge C.20.c.55 broken by enemy shellfire about 1600 hrs but was subsequently repaired	
	8/11		Enemy movement in HERINNES less than usual. Enemy suspected of preparing to evacuate. Patrol sent out at 09.00 hrs. was fired on by three M.Gs. only. Post established in C.20.d.C.21.c.05.45. Two patrols sent out at 1400 hrs almost reached the village but were held up by fire from 3 M.Gs. which continued to fire till 20.30 hrs. At 20.30 hrs the Battalion crossed the ESCAUT R. and advance guard entered HERINNES at 21.00 hrs without encountering opposition. Time extended	
	9/11		02.00 hrs to 9/11. C.23.c.2.16 C.28.b.3.6. One enemy M.G. captured during the above operations.	

Army Form C. 2118.

WAR DIARY
or
INTELLIGENCE SUMMARY.
(Erase heading not required.)

Instructions regarding War Diaries and Intelligence Summaries are contained in F. S. Regs., Part II. and the Staff Manual respectively. Title pages will be prepared in manuscript.

Place	Date	Hour	Summary of Events and Information	Remarks and references to Appendices
	9/11		At 0600 hours the Battalion continued to advance via CHEMIN VERT, BUTOR, MOLEMBAIX to LA BACOTTERIE D28b and D28d. At 08.30 hrs an enemy field gun was captured at D27c84. At 08.45 hrs	
	10/11		At 0700 hrs the advance was continued. Bn was established E25d (HAUT REJET) to K2c. A platoon of v/gs cyclists attached to h Battn reached Railway in F26 and L2 At 14.30 hrs. Battalion was withdrawn from attack (on withdrawal of 40th Divn) and advance guard took to Billets at CHEMIN VERT. Battn. marched back to Billets at CHEMIN VERT.	
	11/11		Battn. cleaning up, kit inspection & checking	
	12/11		Battn. marched from CHEMIN VERT to billets at HERINNES.	

Army Form C. 2118.

WAR DIARY
or
INTELLIGENCE SUMMARY.
(Erase heading not required.)

Instructions regarding War Diaries and Intelligence Summaries are contained in F. S. Regs., Part II. and the Staff Manual respectively. Title pages will be prepared in manuscript.

Place	Date	Hour	Summary of Events and Information	Remarks and references to Appendices
	13/11		Battalion inspected by Commanding Officer. Bathing & change of underclothing.	
	14/11		Training resumed	
	15/11		Training continued	
	16/11		Battalion left HERRINNES and marched to CROIX (Sheet 36 L.9d.) Bivouac in CROIX town. Bn HQ. L.9d.7.6.	
	17/11		Church parade in Factory L.10.c.1.4. at 10.15 a.m.	
	18/11		Educational classes commenced. Held daily from 1400 hrs to 2000 hrs. Instruction given by Officers W.t Officers	

Army Form C. 2118.

WAR DIARY
INTELLIGENCE SUMMARY.
(Erase heading not required.)

Place	Date	Hour	Summary of Events and Information	Remarks and references to Appendices
	18/11 to 20/11		and NCOs of the Battalion in the following subjects:- French, Elementary Mathematics, Motor Engineering, Agricultural Science, Poultry-keeping, Book-keeping, Shorthand, Business methods, Accountancy, Building Construction, Music & Singing, Magnetism & Electricity, Farming, Carpentry and Freehand Drawing. Sports. Lochee teams, Tug of War team, Concert party and Boxing Ring instituted. Training daily. Cross country run for whole of Batt. 26/11.	
	25/11		Battalion attended Brigade Inspection - March Past on Brigade Parade Ground.	

LT-COL
COMMANDING 12TH BN. N. STAFFS REGT.

CONFIDENTIAL

12th Bn. NORTH STAFFORD REGT. 987

WAR DIARY

Vol. VII

From:- 1st Dec. 18
To:- 31st Dec. 18

WAR DIARY
INTELLIGENCE SUMMARY
(Erase heading not required.)

Army Form C. 2118.

Place	Date	Hour	Summary of Events and Information	Remarks and references to Appendices
CROIX	1/12.		CHURCH PARADES	
		09.30	Church of England service in English Church.	
		10.30	Nonconformist service in Cinema	
		11-30	Mass for R.C. in CROIX Church.	
	2/12.	0900	Billets inspected by Commanding Officer	
		0930	Batt. parade for running in Brigade Cross-country run.	
	3/12.	0900	Battalion attended Brigade Parade for inspection by Brigade Commander	
	4/12	0900	Battalion parade to march to NECHIN for inspection by Divisional Commander. Inspection cancelled owing to bad weather.	
	5/12.	0845	Practice ceremonial parade on Brigade parade ground.	
	6/12	0900	Battn marched to Grande Aupes ROUBAIX to attend Divisional Boxing Competition.	

WAR DIARY
or
INTELLIGENCE SUMMARY.
(Erase heading not required.)

Army Form C. 2118.

Place	Date	Hour	Summary of Events and Information	Remarks and references to Appendices
	7/12	0900	Battalion attend Divisional Boxing Competition	
	8/12	0845	All boys parade for singing and inspection by OC Commanders in preparation for afternoon parade.	
		1145	Church of England service in Cinema Hall	
		1030	Non-conformist service in Cinema Hall	
			Jews service in synagogue Rue de Blanpa Roubaix	
		1130	Roman Catholic Mass in CROIX CHURCH	
		1330	Brigade Parade Church Decoration Rewards presented by Divisional Commander	
	9/12	0915	Battalion parade for drill. One Platoon Musketry.	
		1115	Billets inspected by Commanding Officer	
	10/12	0740	Battalion parade to march to NECHIN for inspection by Divisional Commander	

Army Form C. 2118.

WAR DIARY
or
INTELLIGENCE SUMMARY.
(Erase heading not required.)

Instructions regarding War Diaries and Intelligence Summaries are contained in F. S. Regs., Part II. and the Staff Manual respectively. Title pages will be prepared in manuscript.

Place	Date	Hour	Summary of Events and Information	Remarks and references to Appendices
	11/12.	930	Kit inspection by Companies.	
	12/12.	930	Battn parade for drill. One platoon Musketry.	
	13/12	930	Battn parade for drill	
	14/12.	0925	Battalion parade to march to NECHIN for inspection by Corps Commander. Cancelled owing to bad weather.	
	15/12.	0900	Ninety two men per Coy parade and march to GRANDE CIRQUE ROUBAIX for Divisional Inter-denominational service at 1030 hours.	
		1115	Inter-denominational service in Cinema Hall CROIX for all ranks not attending Divisional service.	
		1130	Roman Catholics attend Mass at CROIX Church.	
		0930	Jewish faith, parade to march to ROUBAIX for service at Synagogue 61 RUE-DES-CHAMPS.	

Army Form C. 2118.

WAR DIARY
or
INTELLIGENCE SUMMARY.
(Erase heading not required.)

Instructions regarding War Diaries and Intelligence
Summaries are contained in F.S. Regs., Part II.
and the Staff Manual respectively. Title pages
will be prepared in manuscript.

Place	Date	Hour	Summary of Events and Information	Remarks and references to Appendices
	16/12	0900	Batln parade for Drill	
		1100	Arms drill ½ hour for all men not attending educational classes.	
	17/12	0725	Batln parade and march to NECHIN for inspection by Bgde Commanders.	
	18/12	0930	Parade by Companies for drill & P.T. in factory	
	19/12	0930	Batn parade in factory for close order drill	
		1030	Billets inspected by Commanding Officer.	
	20/12	0930	Batln parade for drill	
		1100	Arms drill 1 hour for all men not attending Classes.	
	21/12	0900	Batln parade for drill.	

WAR DIARY
or
INTELLIGENCE SUMMARY.
(Erase heading not required.)

Army Form C. 2118.

Place	Date	Hour	Summary of Events and Information	Remarks and references to Appendices
	22/12	1010	Nonconformist Service in Cinema	
		1045	Church of England Service in Cinema.	
		1130	R.Cs Mass at CROIX CHURCH	
		930	Jewish Faith parade to march to ROUBAIX for service in ROUBAIX.	
	23/12	0900	Parade for drill	
	24/12	0900	Bath parade for Route March.	
	25/12	9.15 to 0930	Voluntary Divine Services Church of England & Nonconformists.	
		1230	Dinners inspected by Commanding Officer	

Army Form C. 2118.

WAR DIARY
or
INTELLIGENCE SUMMARY.
(Erase heading not required.)

Instructions regarding War Diaries and Intelligence Summaries are contained in F. S. Regs., Part II. and the Staff Manual respectively. Title pages will be prepared in manuscript.

Place	Date	Hour	Summary of Events and Information	Remarks and references to Appendices
	26/12.		Football Matches in morning & afternoon.	
	27/12.	09:30	Batln parade for drill and P.T.	
	28/12.	09:00	Batln parade for drill & P.T.	
		10:30	Horses, Wheels, & Transport inspected by Commanding Officer.	
		11:00	Kit inspection by Companies.	
	29/12.	09:30	Jewish Lads paraded for service at ROUBAIX CINEMA.	
		09:50	Nonconformists parade for service in Bureau.	
		10:30	Church of England parade for service in CROIX CHURCH.	
		11:15	R.C. parade for Mass at CROIX CHURCH.	
	30/12.	09:30	Parade by Coys for fighting order inspection.	
	31/12.	09:00	Battn parade for Route March.	
		09:30	Drills inspected by the Commanding Officer.	

J.F. Seymour Major
Comdg 12th North Staff Regt.

Army Form C. 2118.

12 N Staff

WAR DIARY

INTELLIGENCE SUMMARY.

(Erase heading not required.)

Instructions regarding War Diaries and Intelligence Summaries are contained in F. S. Regs., Part II. and the Staff Manual respectively. Title pages will be prepared in manuscript.

Place	Date	Hour	Summary of Events and Information	Remarks and references to Appendices
In the field	1/1/19	9.00 to 10.00	Route march	
		10.00 to 10.30	Arms Drill	
		10.30 to 11.00	Lecture Military Hygiene	
	2/1/19	09.00 to 15.00	Bathing	
			C.O's lecture on Pozn. Bellum Army	Brigade Inter. Company match football
	3/1/19	10.15 to 10.45	Divisional Commanders Inspection	
	4/1/19	9.00 to 9.30	Physical Training	Brigade Inter. Company match football
		9.30 to 10.00	Steady Drill	
		10.00 to 12.00	Medical Inspection	
	5/1/19		Divine service:-	
		10.00	Church of England	
		10.00	Roman Catholic	
		9.30	Church South	

Army Form C. 2118.

WAR DIARY
or
INTELLIGENCE SUMMARY.
(Erase heading not required.)

Instructions regarding War Diaries and Intelligence Summaries are contained in F. S. Regs., Part II. and the Staff Manual respectively. Title pages will be prepared in manuscript.

Place	Date	Hour	Summary of Events and Information	Remarks and references to Appendices
	6/9/19	09.00 to 09.30	Physical training	
		10.00 to 10.30	Entire Drill	
			C.O's Lecture on Post-Bellum army	
			Brigade Inter Company match football	
	7/9/19	09.00 to 15.00	Baths	
			Guard Drill. Boxing.	
	8/9/19	09.00 to 10.00	Route March.	
		10.00 to 10.30	Guard Drill.	
			Lecture.	
			Brigade Inter Company match football	E.R.H.L.
	9/9/19	09.30 to 10.30	Battalion Drill	
		10.00 to 10.30	Guard Drill	
			Lecture	
			Brigade Inter Company match football	
	10/9/19	09.00 to 10.00	Physical training	
		10.00 to 10.30	Arts Drill	
			Rifles Inspected by C.O.	
			Training for Patts Boxing Tournament	
	11/9/19	09.00	Practice for Corps Commanders Church Parade	
		09.15	Lecture by Lieut Nelson (Demobilization)	
			Brigade Inter Company match football	
	12/9/19	09.00	Corps Commanders Church Parade.	

WAR DIARY

INTELLIGENCE SUMMARY

(Erase heading not required.)

Army Form C. 2118.

Place	Date	Hour	Summary of Events and Information	Remarks and references to Appendices
	13/1/19	09.00 to 10.00	P.T. and Bayonet fighting	
		10.00 to 10.15	musketry	
		10.15 to 10.30	Arms drill with fixed bayonets	
		10.30 to 14.30	Guard drill	
		14.00	No 16 platoon to Rifle Range	
		05.20		
	14/1/19	09.00	Practice for trooping of the Colours	
		09.00 to 10.00	Remainder of Batt. Route march.	Inter platoon football match
		11.00	Inspection of Billets by C.O.	
			No 16 platoon to Rifles Range	
	15/1/19	09.15	Practice for Trooping the Colours	O. Coy. Whist Drive
		09.00 to 09.30	Remainder of Batt. P.T.	Brigade Football League
		09.30 to 10.00	musketry	B Coy v D Coy.
		10.00 to 10.30	Arms drill with fixed bayonets	
	16/1/19	09.15	Practice for trooping the Colours	Batts. Boxing Tournament at 6.p.1
		09.15	Remainder of Batts. paraded on Rec Parade ground	Inter platoon football final
		08.20	No 16 platoon Range	
	17/1/19	09.15	Practice for trooping the Colours	Batts. Boxing Tournament [illegible]
		09.15	Remainder of Batt. paraded on Rec Parade ground	Batts. concert Bde Football League x coy v D Coy
		08.30	No 16 platoon Range	

WAR DIARY

INTELLIGENCE SUMMARY

(Erase heading not required.)

Army Form C. 2118.

Place	Date	Hour	Summary of Events and Information	Remarks and references to Appendices
	18/1/19	08.30	No 16 Platoon Range	
		09.15	Practice for Trooping the Colours	
		09.00	Remainder of Bn Bath parades Bn Parade Ground	
		09.20	No 16 Platoon Range	
		11.00 to 12.00	Medical Inspection	
	19/1/19	09.25	Divine Service Church of England	
		10.25	Nonconformists	
		11.15	Roman Catholics	
		09.30	Jewish Faith	
	20/1/19	08.45	Practice ceremonial Parade for Consecration of Colours	Bee football League A Coy v. T. M. Bty.
	21/1/19	09.40	Presentation and Consecration of Colours	
		14.00 to 16.00	Bathing	
	22/1/19	09.30 & 10.15	Lecture by Commanding Officer	No 16 Platoon Range Bathing 09.30 to 15.00
	23/1/19	09.30	Parade	
			No 16 Platoon Range	
		10.00	Concert party parade	
	24/1/19	08.00	No 16 Platoon Range. Remainder of Batt. P.T. and run lasting one hour.	

Army Form C. 2118.

WAR DIARY
~~INTELLIGENCE SUMMARY~~

Instructions regarding War Diaries and Intelligence Summaries are contained in F. S. Regs., Part II. and the Staff Manual respectively. Title pages will be prepared in manuscript.

(Erase heading not required.)

Place	Date	Hour	Summary of Events and Information	Remarks and references to Appendices
	25/1/19	09.30	Lecture by Commanding Officer	
	26/1/19		Divine Service	
		09.25	Church of England	
		09.50	Nonconformists	
		11.20	Roman Catholic	
		09.30	Jewish faith	
	27/1/19	09.30	Batt. Parade for clearing Roads of Snow	
		09.30	No 16 platoon to Range	
	28/1/19	08.00	No 16 platoon a.R.a Competition	
		08.30	Remainder of Batt. clearing roads	
	29/1/19	08.30	Parade for clearing Roads of Snow	
	30/1/19	08.30	No 16 platoon a.R.a Competition	
		08.30	Remainder of Batt. parade for road clearing (snow)	
	31/1/19	08.30	Batt. Parade for clearing Roads of Snow. Lecture by by Colo. on War Savings certificates	

E.D.O'Connor.
Lt-Col.
Commanding 12th Bn. K. Stafford Regt.

CONFIDENTIAL.

989

12TH Bn. N. STAFFS. REGT.

WAR DIARY

VOL IX.

From 1/2/19
To 28/2/19.

Army Form C. 2118.

WAR DIARY
or
INTELLIGENCE SUMMARY.
(Erase heading not required.)

Instructions regarding War Diaries and Intelligence Summaries are contained in F. S. Regs. Part II. and the Staff Manual respectively. Title pages will be prepared in manuscript.

Place	Date	Hour	Summary of Events and Information	Remarks and references to Appendices
CROIX NORD	1/2 1919	1200	Visit by Divisional Commander	
		0900	Battalion bathing	
		1800		
	2/2	0930	Divine Service	
		1000	Hymn - Catholic's	
		1000	Church of England	
		1000	Wesleyan & Nonconformists	
			Jewish faith	
	3/2	0900	Battalion clearing roads of snow	
	4/2	0800	Battalion bathing	
		1200		
	5/2	0900	Parade for P T	
		1000	Lecture on Demobilization and Discipline	
	6/2	0900	Battalion parade for P T	
			Lecture on War Savings Certificates	
	7/2	0900	Battalion parade for clearing roads of snow	
	8/2	0900	Battalion parade for clearing roads of snow	

Army Form C. 2118.

WAR DIARY
or
INTELLIGENCE SUMMARY
(Erase heading not required.)

Instructions regarding War Diaries and Intelligence Summaries are contained in F. S. Regs., Part II. and the Staff Manual respectively. Title pages will be prepared in manuscript.

Place	Date	Hour	Summary of Events and Information	Remarks and references to Appendices
Brias	9/2/19	10.00	Divine Service. United Service Church of England Nonconformist	
		11.30	Roman Catholics	
	10/2/19	09.00	Both clearing roads of snow.	
	11/2/19	09.45	Lecture in Routaine	
	12/2/19	09.30	Parade of heads for inspection	
	13/2/19	8.30	Battalion parade in transport lines for fatigue. Battalions formed into 3 companies	
		12.00	Parade of employed men	7/05 1, 2 and 3
		15.00	Parade of remainder of employed men.	ERWE
	14/2/19	09.00	Battalion parade for cleaning billets	
	15/2/19	09.00	Battalion parade in transport lines for fatigue	
	16/2/19	10.00	Divine Service. Divine Service Church of England Nonconformist	
		11.15	Roman Catholics	
	17/2/19	05.00	Bathing	
		10.30		

Army Form C. 2118.

WAR DIARY
or
INTELLIGENCE SUMMARY.
(Erase heading not required.)

Instructions regarding War Diaries and Intelligence Summaries are contained in F. S. Regs., Part II. and the Staff Manual respectively. Title pages will be prepared in manuscript.

Place	Date	Hour	Summary of Events and Information	Remarks and references to Appendices
Loure	18/2/19	09.00	Battalion parade cleaning billets	
	19/2/19	08.00	Battalion parade for fatigue in transport lines	
	20/2/19	10.30 12.00	Battalion Bathing	
	21/2/19	09.00	Battalion parade for fatigue in transport lines	
	22/2/19	09.00	Battalion parade for fatigue in transport lines	Show
	23/2/19	10.00 11.30	Divine Service Church of England and Nonconformist. Roman Catholics	
	24/2/19	09.00 09.45 09.45	O.J. Drill order inspection. Brigade Inter. Battalion football Match. 4th vs 13th East Lancashire Regt. Result. M Staff 3 goals. 4 hours. 2"	
	25/2/19	09.30	Battalion parade for Arms drill. Brigade Inter Battalion football Match. 4th vs 13th Royal Inniskilling Fusiliers. Result M Staff 1 goal. Inniskillings 2 goals.	

Army Form C. 2118.

WAR DIARY
or
INTELLIGENCE SUMMARY.
(Erase heading not required.)

Instructions regarding War Diaries and Intelligence Summaries are contained in F. S. Regs. Part II. and the Staff Manual respectively. Title pages will be prepared in manuscript.

Place	Date 1919	Hour	Summary of Events and Information	Remarks and references to Appendices
CROIX NORD	26/2	0930	Battalion parade for drill	
	27/2	0930	Battalion parade for drill	Ehr2
	28/2	0930	Battalion parade for drill	

E.D.Evans.
LT-COL.
COMMANDING 12TH BN. N. STAFFS REGT.

CONFIDENTIAL

12th Battalion North Staffs Regt.

Vol 10

WAR DIARY

VOL X

From 1/3/19
To 30/3/19

Army Form C. 2118.

WAR DIARY
or
INTELLIGENCE SUMMARY
(Erase heading not required.)

Instructions regarding War Diaries and Intelligence Summaries are contained in F. S. Regs., Part II. and the Staff Manual respectively. Title pages will be prepared in manuscript.

Place	Date	Hour	Summary of Events and Information	Remarks and references to Appendices
Crecy France	1.3.19.	09.50	Divine Service	
		11.20	C of E	
		09.50	Roman Catholic (Civic Church)	
			Nonconformist	
	2.3.19	09.30	Battalion parade for Drill	
	3.3.19	09.30	Battalion parade for Drill	
	4.3.19	09.30	Battalion Bathing	
	5.3.19	09.30	Battalion parade for Drill	
	6.3.19	09.30	Battalion parade for P.T. & Medical Inspection	Nil
	7.3.19	09.30	Battalion Route March	
	8.3.19	09.30	Divine Service C of E & Nonconformist	
		11.30	Roman Catholic (Civic Church)	
	9.3.19	09.30	Battalion parade for P.T.	
	10.3.19	09.30	Battalion parade for Drill	
	11.3.19	09.30	Bathing	
	12.3.19	09.30	Battalion parade for P.T.	
	13.3.19	—	Battalion parade for Cleaning equipment & Billets	

Army Form C. 2118.

WAR DIARY
or
INTELLIGENCE SUMMARY.
(Erase heading not required.)

Instructions regarding War Diaries and Intelligence Summaries are contained in F. S. Regs., Part II. and the Staff Manual respectively. Title pages will be prepared in manuscript.

Place	Date	Hour	Summary of Events and Information	Remarks and references to Appendices
Crace France	14.3.19		Battalion parade for Commanding Officer's Inspection	
	15.3.19	09.30	Divine Service	
			United Service C of E's Nonconformists	
		11.30	Roman Catholic Church	
	16.3.19	09.30	Battalion Parade for Drill	
	17.3.19	09.30	Battalion Parade for Drill	
	18.3.19		Battalion Parade for Baths	
	19.3.19	10.00	Battalion Parade for P.T.	
	20.3.19	09.30	Battalion Parade for Drill	
	21.3.19	—	Cleaning of Billets	
	22.3.19		Divine Service	
			C of E's Nonconformists United Service	
		09.30	Roman Catholic Church	
	23.3.19	09.30	Battalion Parade for P.T.	
	24.3.19	09.30	Battalion Parade for Drill	
	25.3.19	09.30	Battalion Parade for Baths	

Army Form C. 2118.

WAR DIARY
of
INTELLIGENCE SUMMARY.
(Erase heading not required.)

Instructions regarding War Diaries and Intelligence
Summaries are contained in F. S. Regs., Part II.
and the Staff Manual respectively. Title pages
will be prepared in manuscript.

Place	Date	Hour	Summary of Events and Information	Remarks and references to Appendices
Croix France	26.3.19	09.30	Battalion parade for drill	
	27.3.19	09.30	Cleaning of Equipment & Breeches	
	28.3.19	06.00	All men with exception of Cadre leave for 10 M Corps	
	29.3.19	09.30	Divine Services	
		11.30	C/of E & Nonconformist Roman Catholics Cadre Church	
	30.3.19		Commanding Officers inspection of Cadre	
	31.3.19		Cleaning of Equipment & Clothes for G.O.C. inspection	

RBConnor Lt-Col.
COMMANDING 12TH BN. N. STAFFS REGT.

War Diary

12 Bn N. Staff. Regt

Month of April, 1919

12th Bn North Staffordshire Regt. Vol XI

Army Form C. 2118.

WAR DIARY
or
INTELLIGENCE SUMMARY.

(Erase heading not required.)

Place	Date	Hour	Summary of Events and Information	Remarks and references to Appendices
Crown	1-4-19 to 30-4-19		Cadre Strength Only. Guards & Fatigues. Bathing Parade Monday & Wednesday. Divine Service each Sunday. Cadres to office League Matches Monday & Wednesday & Saturday. Billet Inspection Daily. Kit Inspection Weekly. Lewis Guns, Revolvers, Rifles inspected by armourer, 29.4.19.	

F.J. Senior Major
COMMANDING 12TH BN. N. STAFFS REGT.

13th Bn North Staffordshire Regt. Vol XII

WAR DIARY
or
INTELLIGENCE SUMMARY

Army Form C. 2118.

WO/1/29/13

Place	Date	Hour	Summary of Events and Information	Remarks and references to Appendices
CROIX	1.5.19 to 25.5.19		Cadre Strength (36) only. Guards & fatigues. Bathing each Monday & Wednesday. Divine services each Sunday. Rifle inspection daily. Kit inspection weekly.	Nil
	26.5.19		Entrained at Croix for Dunkirk to proceed to England.	
	2.6.19		Embarked at Dunkirk for Southampton	
	3.6.19		Arrived at Southampton	
	4.6.19		Proceeded to St Lucia Barks Bordon for Disposal	

W.E. Woodcock Capt MAO/
for

www.ingramcontent.com/pod-product-compliance
Lightning Source LLC
Chambersburg PA
CBHW081557160426
43191CB00011B/1953